SMITHSONIAN INSTI

BUREAU OF AMERICAN I

The Northern Arapaho Flat Pipe and the Ceremony of Covering the Pipe

By JOHN G. CARTER

Chapter from BULLETIN 119, Bureau of American Ethnology

Anthropological Papers, No. 2

UNITED STATES

GOVERNMENT PRINTING OFFICE

WASHINGTON: 1938

CONTENTS

ILLUSTRATIONS

THE NORTHERN ARAPAHO FLAT PIPE AND THE CEREMONY OF COVERING THE PIPE

By John G. Carter

Introduction

The Flat Pipe (sĕicha, Mooney, 1896, p. 959; säeitca[n], Kroeber, p. 308) is the tribal medicine of the Arapaho, and its keeper is always a member of the northern band of that tribe. The word medicine, as here employed, is the word which white men have applied to those objects or ceremonies of the North American Indian which either contain in themselves, or produce by their performance, supernatural power. This supernatural power is sought and applied by the Indian not only to the purpose of healing the sick but also to obtain control of natural forces, success in hunting, good luck, strength, long life, and safety and victory in the hour of battle. The Flat Pipe in the Arapaho mythology is really the creator, and is held by the Arapaho in greater veneration than the sun (Dorsey and Kroeber, 2). Its present custodian (1936) is Oscar White, a full-blood Arapaho Indian, who lives on the Wind River Reservation at Ethete, Wyo.

The Flat Pipe has been discussed by Mooney (1896, pp. 956, 959–961, 1063), by Dorsey (pp. 191–212), by Dorsey and Kroeber (pp. 1–6), and by Kroeber (pp. 291–292, 294, 296–300, 308–310, 359–361).

The outlines of the creation myth, in which the Flat Pipe takes a prominent part, are known. This myth is in the custody of the pipe keeper. No white man has ever recorded the myth in its entirety. Fragments of the myth have been obtained from Arapaho who had heard it, and know it but imperfectly. These fragments are sometimes contradictory in their details. Those who know the myth, or who have heard it, are forbidden to tell it (Kroeber, p. 309). In outline the myth recites that in the beginning there was nothing but water. Some say that a man and his wife and son, with the Flat Pipe supported on its stand of four poles, floated alone on the water, and that "the grandfather" took pity on them. Others say that a man walked alone on the water carrying the Flat Pipe and sought land on which to rest his pipe. In this situation the man, or the grandfather (the fragments contradict each other), sent animals down into the water to bring up land from the bottom with which to make the earth. The turtle finally succeeds in bringing up enough earth, and with this the man, or the grandfather, makes the land. The mountains, rivers, trees and grass, the animals, and finally man are all made by this first being. The Arapaho are made, and the maker gives the Flat Pipe to the Arapaho. The myth implies that either the world was made at the Flat Pipe's request or because of the Flat Pipe, and in order to provide a place on which the Flat Pipe could rest (Dorsey and Kroeber, pp. 1–6; Dorsey, pp. 191–212).

In 1892 Mooney was refused permission to see the Flat Pipe (1896, p. 961). In 1900 Kroeber observed the Flat Pipe bundle hung from its stand of four poles in the northern Arapaho sun dance lodge   At the time of Kroeber's observation it was said that the Flat Pipe was removed from its bundle and was in the keeping of the pledger of the sun dance, or in the back of the lodge behind the pledger, and that the Pipe was taken back to the bundle by the keeper at the end of the sun dance (Kroeber, pp. 291–292, 296–300). But it is also stated on reliable authority that the Pipe remains in its bundle during the sun dance (Friday).[1] The Flat Pipe has been seen by Dr. John Roberts. Weasel Bear was its keeper at that time (Mooney, 1896, 961; Friday). Mr. Hastings, a missionary, gave the feast for the Pipe, and with his wife and daughter saw the Pipe. It is believed that a Dr. Brown saw the Pipe, but informant is not sure of this. Dr. Tyler, formerly missionary in charge of the Episcopal mission at Ethete, Wyo., saw the Pipe (Friday); and was permitted to lift and handle it (Fontenelle). Mr. Roy H. Balcom, of New York, and Dr. Corey saw the Pipe and gave the feast for the Pipe (Friday). A careful search has been made of the card index catalogs of the Library of Congress and the Library of the Bureau of American Ethnology, Smithsonian Institution, in order to ascertain if any of the above named have published papers on the Flat Pipe, and no reference to any such publications has been found. If there be any oversight in giving credit where credit is due in regard to papers published on the Flat Pipe the oversight is regretted.

The writer is informed that he is the first white man to take the part of "he who covers the Pipe" in the ceremony here described (Friday), and it is to be noted that when reference is made to "he

---

[1] The following information was received in a letter from Harlow E. Burt, Chief Clerk, Shoshoni Agency, Fort Washakie, Wyo., dated June 26, 1937: "Your old friend Oscar White passed to his happy reward February 16th last. His daughter, Hanna Brown, has the medal you sent to her father. She told me they prize it highly and would keep it among members of their family. She also has the Arapaho peace pipe. It has not been determined as yet who will be chosen as permanent keeper of the sacred emblem. Mrs. Brown did say that Luke Smith, stepson of Oscar White, was a likely candidate. You wish to know 'if the peace pipe was exposed at some time during the Arapaho sun dance.' The answer is no. My source of information is Mr. Friday, Mr. Whiteman, Hannah Brown, and Domic Oldman, all important members of the Araphao tribe."

Friday, on a visit to Washington, D. C., in July 1937, stated that Luke Smith (Wolf Lung) had succeeded Oscar White as keeper of the Flat Pipe.

who covers the Pipe" in this paper, the reference is to the author of this paper, and all matters here related, and not credited to others, fell directly under his observation.

The following persons have been of the greatest assistance in giving information in regard to the Flat Pipe and in making it possible to see the Pipe and take part in the ceremony of covering the Pipe: Robert Friday, a full-blood Arapaho, and chairman of the Arapaho tribal council; Mrs. Robert Friday; Dr. John Roberts, missionary of the Episcopal Church among the Arapaho and Shoshoni since 1882, and still actively engaged in that work among them; Shave Head, a full-blood Arapaho Indian; Oscar White, keeper of the Flat Pipe; Luke Smith, assistant keeper of the Flat Pipe; Victor Fontenelle, an Omaha Indian, private secretary to the superintendent of the reservation; and Forrest R. Stone, superintendent of the Wind River Reservation, who gave most valuable assistance in making contacts with and gaining the confidence and good will of Arapaho Indians. Robert Friday, who acted as negotiator, informant, sponsor, coach, instructor, and interpreter in the ceremony here described, checked over the notes taken on the ceremony and on the Flat Pipe and made corrections and additions where needed.

THE ARAPAHO

The Arapaho are an important tribe of the Algonquian linguistic stock. Several hundred years ago this tribe was located in western Minnesota. According to their traditions they were then an agricultural and sedentary people. They gradually migrated south and west from their original habitat, allying themselves with the Cheyenne at the time of their migration. Early in the nineteenth century they acquired horses. Their migration, acquisition of horses, and their emergence into the buffalo country led them to abandon their agricultural habits and culture and adopt the culture of the plains or buffalo-hunting tribes. The reason for their migration is unknown. At an early period in this migration the first division of the Arapaho occurred, when a band, later known as the Gros Ventres of the Prairie, left the Arapaho, and subsequently allied themselves with the Piegan tribe of the Blackfeet Nation. These Gros Ventres now reside on the Fort Belknap Reservation in north central Montana. The main body of the Arapaho journeyed on to the Black Hills, where they parted company with the Cheyenne, with whom, however, they continued ever after to have close alliance and friendship. The Arapaho then proceeded to the headwaters of the Missouri, but driven from that country by the Piegans and other Indians, they then found their way to the headwaters of the Platte, a part of the tribe ranging south to the headwaters of the Arkansas. In 1849 the great overland route, which followed the North Platte, permanently divided the buffalo into the northern and southern herds, and these herds were never again united. It is believed that this led to the last division of the Arapaho.[2] That part of the tribe now known as the Southern Arapaho who now have a reservation with the Cheyenne in Oklahoma, followed the southern herd along the Arkansas. That part of the tribe now known as the Northern Arapaho, who now reside on the Wind River Reservation in Wyoming, remained with the northern herd north of the Platte. The Arapaho recognize the northern tribe in Wyoming as the mother tribe, and it is this tribe of the Arapaho who retained custody of the tribal medicine known as the Flat Pipe (Mooney, 1896, pp. 954–1023; 1907, pp. 72–74; Clark, pp. 38–43; Strong, p. 37).

POSITION OF THE FLAT PIPE AMONG THE ARAPAHO

The Flat Pipe is looked upon by the Arapaho as an exceedingly holy object, and is held in the highest possible veneration and respect. The Christianized Arapaho refer to it as "the chariot of God," because, they say, when a man looks upon the Pipe his "shadow" is at once transported to "the home." By "shadow" is meant the soul or spirit, and "the home" refers to the place where the Arapaho journey after death (Roberts). In the old days the Pipe was considered too holy to be carried on horseback or travois. The keeper then carried the Pipe, wrapped in its bundle, with the four poles which formed the stand for the bundle when at rest, and proceeded afoot when the camp moved (Mooney, 1896, p. 960; Roberts). As the bundle is about 2 feet long, and the poles are about 5 feet long, the keeper was obliged to walk slowly, and no great distance could be covered in a day's march. When encamped the camp circle formed around the keeper's lodge. When on the march the camp formed around the keeper, and thus the people were kept close together. This was a good thing because it kept them from straggling or scattering when moving through hostile territory (Roberts). The keeper, when the camp was on the march, walked under guard (Mooney, 1896, p. 960).

In the Northern Arapaho sun dance lodge the Flat Pipe, wrapped in its bundle, is brought into the lodge, and is there suspended from its stand of four poles (Kroeber, p. 291; Friday). The four poles are arranged like the poles of a tipi or a lodge, and from the point where they are bound together near their tips the bundle is secured by a thong and hangs free. The pipe bundle, suspended from this stand, was

---

[2] Robert Friday while visiting Washington in July 1937 made the following comment with reference to this statement: That the old men of the Northern Arapaho had told him that the Northern and Southern Arapaho were originally different tribes, and the southern tribe spoke a different language from the northern tribe when they first met. That originally the southern tribe lived to the south of the Northern Arapaho, and had horses. The Northern Arapaho had good lodge poles in their country, and traded these for the horses of the southern tribe, the trade being carried on in the neighborhood of Fort Dodge. As a result of this commerce the southern tribe, according to Friday's informants, picked up the language of the Northern Arapaho, and became known as Southern Arapaho. Thus there was an amalgamation of the two tribes, and not a division of Southern Arapaho from the parent stock, according to Friday.

sometimes placed in front of two or more of the sun dancers (Kroeber, p. 292). Food was offered to the pipe bundle by the dancers in the sun dance lodge (Kroeber, p. 296). The dancers also touched the pipe bundle and cried over it (Kroeber, p. 299). All those wishing to do so make offerings to the Flat Pipe bundle in the sun dance lodge. But only offerings of felt cloth or of sun shells are exposed (Mrs. Friday). It is supposed that this means that only these offerings are used to cover the pipe bundle, or to be exhibited as offerings. Offerings of cloth, other than felt, are retained by the keeper and may be given by him to the different members of his family for the women to make up into dresses. But this cloth, when so used, cannot be handled like ordinary cloth. All scraps left over from the making of these dresses must be wrapped up into a small wad or bundle, and the wad or bundle either burned, or thrown into a stream of running water. Dresses or other garments made of this cloth, when worn out, cannot be disposed of in the same manner as ordinary clothing, but must be bundled up, and the bundle must be either burned or cast into a running stream (Mrs. Friday).

When a feast is prepared in honor of the Flat Pipe the women who help prepare the feast, and carry the food to the tent or lodge in which the ceremony is given, feel amply compensated for their work, as they are permitted, at the proper time, to come into the place where the ceremony is occurring, and see the Flat Pipe and touch it with the sole of their bare right foot. They are also allowed to partake of some of the food, which is blessed, offered, and eaten in honor of the Pipe, and they feel amply rewarded for their work by the opportunity afforded them of obtaining these blessings (Friday).

The person who gives the ceremony of covering the Pipe is known as "he who covers the Pipe" or "he who worships the Pipe" or "the coverer" (Shave Head; Friday), and acquires considerable prestige and standing among the Arapaho by so doing. Very few Arapaho can give the ceremony, and comparatively few have done so. Robert Friday once gave the ceremony in order to obtain recovery from illness of his daughter (Friday). "He who covers the Pipe" by giving this ceremony not only gains blessings of health, long life, good fortune, and security for himself and his family, but also permits others to share in these blessings at his expense, since all who wish to do so may come forward at the proper time and touch the Pipe with the sole of their bare right foot, and thereby gain from the Pipe strength, and all of these other blessings. The food which is blessed and eaten in honor of the Pipe is also in great demand. The partaking of it is regarded in the same light as communion among Christians (Friday). As an abundance of food is provided, and comparatively little is consumed at the ceremony, the remainder of the food is distributed to the village or carried home by those present at the ceremony. Thus the greatest number possible of the people may eat the blessed food, and when the ceremony is given a great number of people profit by it at no cost to themselves.

It is said that during the tenure of the last keeper, before Oscar White, the Pipe sealed itself up. When the former keeper had occasion to open the bundle and expose the Pipe he found the bowl of the Pipe sealed with a tallow plug. This, the keeper declared, had been done by the Pipe, and not by him, for the reason that the people had become so wicked that the Pipe refused to permit itself to be smoked any longer by them. The keeper also declared that when the people improved their conduct, at some future time, the Pipe would unseal itself (Friday).

Prior to the time that the Pipe was sealed it could be smoked. But the ceremony of smoking the Flat Pipe could only be gone through with at night (Friday). Dr. Roberts, who evidently saw the Pipe after it had been sealed, states that it appears to have been sealed with a pebble, and that the opening of the bowl which is covered by the seal is about the size of a half dollar.

The myth of the origin of the Pipe; of the creation of the earth; information about the contents of the bowl of the Pipe, which holds among other things a grain of corn; the formula for making the incense, as well as the powder with which the woman helper blesses the food; information about the ear of corn in the Pipe bundle, and the turtle, which is part of the Pipe equipment; the history of the different wrappings which make up the Pipe bundle; and all other matters relating to the Pipe and its ceremonies can be told only at night. It takes three nights for the keeper to impart information in regard to the creation and the origin and history of the Pipe. One who wishes to receive this information must make a suitable present to the keeper and abstain from food and water for the 3 days and 3 nights period during which he is receiving the information. He may rest during the day, and receives the information only at night. The last night is the most severe, for it takes the keeper the entire night to get through with all he has to tell (Friday).

REQUIREMENTS FOR OPENING THE FLAT PIPE BUNDLE

By opening the Flat Pipe bundle is meant having the proper ceremony performed whereby the bundle containing the Flat Pipe is unwrapped and the Pipe exposed to view. Anyone who is able to meet the general requirements, make the necessary gifts, and give the feast, may have the ceremony performed and the bundle opened. First of all it is necessary to believe in the Flat Pipe (Friday). Then it is necessary to procure a yard or more of red or blue felt cloth, of a certain quality, with which to "cover the Pipe." As cloth of this kind is no longer carried by the traders, or in the local stores, this is difficult. In the ceremony here described the cloth required had to be purchased at second hand. In addition to the felt cloth five sun shells should be procured. These are circular or oval discs cut from some shell (perhaps abalone) with a pink inner surface, and were formerly much in demand for earrings. They are no longer carried by the traders or in local stores, and could not be obtained for this particular ceremony. Finally it is necessary for "he who covers the Pipe" to provide a feast. The feast must consist of at least five dishes, and the more varieties of food furnished in addition to this the better the feast is considered to be, according to Arapaho standards in regard to this kind of a ceremony. The quantity of food does not appear to matter so much. It is the variety of foods furnished that counts (Friday). Women must be found who will purchase, prepare, and carry the food to the tent or lodge where the ceremony is given. "He who covers the Pipe" must procure a pipe and have it filled with the proper mixture of kinnikinnick and tobacco. This is the pipe he will carry, with the cloth offering wrapped about its stem, to the tent where the ceremony is to take place. A second pipe must be procured, with a bag containing the proper mixture of tobacco and kinnikinnick, for sociable smoking during the ceremony, and this pipe and tobacco must also be carried to the place of the ceremony. In the present ceremony the absence of the five sun shells was compensated for by fastening a bill of modest denomination to the felt cloth offering, in the place where the shells would have been fastened had they been obtainable.

On the present occasion all of the preliminary purchases of food, and the procuring of women assistants, cloth, pipes, and tobacco, and all the negotiations connected with the ceremony were placed in the hands of Robert Friday and Mrs. Friday, who handled everything in the most satisfactory manner. The actual money cost is very moderate. In fact money by itself will get a person nowhere in regard to the Flat Pipe. The proper forms and ceremonies must be gone through and the proper gifts provided. Otherwise the bundle containing the Flat Pipe remains closed. The matter has to be conducted Arapaho fashion or not at all. And even if all the proper gifts can be procured, and the feast provided, it is useless to attempt to see the Pipe unless the confidence, good will, and active support of the Arapaho concerned is first obtained. Arapaho friends, well-wishers, and active supporters are a primary essential. The three things necessary to open the Pipe bundle are therefore: the confidence and help of certain Arapaho; the necessary gifts; and to do it their way.

The Pipe-Covering Ceremony and Feast in Honor of the Pipe

PRELIMINARY CEREMONIES

At the camp of Oscar White, the Pipe keeper, a wall tent has been set up for the ceremony. The door of the tent faces east. Prior to this it is understood that the keeper and his party have taken a sweat bath. Such a sweat bath requires that seven dippers full of water be thrown on the hot stones in the sweat lodge (Shave Head). Luke Smith, assistant keeper, stepson of Oscar White, and his successor in office (Friday), now goes to Oscar White's dwelling, and there removes the Pipe bundle and the four poles which support the bundle, and carries these to the tent prepared for the ceremony. Luke Smith is the only person who is authorized to carry the Pipe bundle and the four poles which are used for its stand (Friday). Oscar White appears to be an old man, and rather feeble.

The stand of four poles, with the bundle attached, is lashed securely by Luke Smith to the west tent pole of the tent where the ceremony is to take place. The poles are placed flat against the west wall of the tent so as not to be in the way. The bundle is hung free from the point of intersection near the ends of the two pairs of poles, whose butts rest on the ground to the north and south of the west tent pole. These poles are between the bundle and the west tent pole and are secured to the tent pole at their point of intersection.

While the Pipe bundle is being placed in the tent the party of "he who covers the Pipe" is forming at the tent of Robert Friday, at which place the food for the feast has been prepared by Mrs. Friday and her women helpers. Friday moved in from his farm, 10 miles distant, and borrowed a tent in Oscar White's camp for this ceremony. Mrs. Friday the day before the ceremony rode 20 miles to town in a wagon to make the necessary purchases of cloth and food, and she and her women helpers have been busy all morning preparing the feast. It is now a few minutes after 11 in the morning and all is in readiness.

PROCESSION OF PARTY OF "HE WHO COVERS THE PIPE" TO TENT OF FLAT PIPE

"He who covers the Pipe" heads the procession. He carries a pipe with a catlinite bowl, filled with a mixture of tobacco and kinnikinnick. Around the wooden stem of this pipe is carefully wrapped the yard of blue felt cloth, which had previously been folded to a convenient size. On the inner side of this cloth, next to the pipestem, has been pinned an offering, in lieu of the five sun shells which should have been placed there, but which could not be obtained. The pipe is held with the right hand forward under the bowl, the bowl being held forward, away from the body, and slanted slightly downward. It is about level with the pit of the stomach. The left hand holds the stem, back near the mouthpiece. The hands are outside the wrapping of the pipe, and holding the wrapping in place around the pipe. The stem of the pipe is slanted to the left of the body, and is held close to the body. On the left of "he who covers the Pipe," and about a foot behind him, stands Robert Friday, who carries a pipe with a black stone bowl, and with it a bag containing a mixture of tobacco and kinnikinnick. Following these two are the wife and daughter of "he who covers the Pipe," who are followed in turn by Mr. and Mrs. Henry Elkin, Vic Fontenelle, and then by Mrs. Friday and 10 women who carry the food for the feast in pots, kettles, pans, and buckets. All the party are bareheaded and stand together in close formation. Friday's tent is south and west of the tent where the ceremony is to take place and distant from it about 100 yards. The party of "he who covers the Pipe" now advances slowly toward the tent prepared for the ceremony. The heads of the two leaders of the party are bowed. The pipe carried by "he who covers the Pipe" is held carefully by him in the manner before described, until the moment of its surrender to the Pipe keeper. While the party is slowly advancing Oscar White proceeds to a point in the rear of the tent where the ceremony is to take place, and standing there summons by name the persons designated as helpers by him, in a loud voice. On arriving near the tent, at a point close to its southeast corner, the party of "he who covers the Pipe" halts. They remain at that position for a few minutes, while the keeper of the Flat Pipe, his helpers and assistants take their places inside the tent. When all is ready a voice calls from the tent for the party to come in. The party now advances to the entrance of the tent, turns west, enters the tent, and crosses to where the Pipe keeper is seated before the suspended bundle. The Pipe keeper faces east. Standing directly in front of the keeper, "he who covers the Pipe" shifts the position of the pipe he carries, without, however, disturbing the cloth wrapping which is around the pipe. The stem of this pipe is swung clockwise, and away from the body, until the mouthpiece points downward toward the Pipe keeper, the bowl being then next to the body of "he who covers the Pipe." The pipe is then passed slowly and carefully toward the keeper, the left hand forward and under the stem near the mouthpiece, and the right hand nearest the body and under the bowl of the pipe. The Pipe keeper takes the pipe from "he who covers the Pipe," without disturbing its cloth wrapping, then removes the wrapping and places it behind him on his right, and lays the pipe he has received across his knees, the bowl to the north. Meantime "he who covers the Pipe" extends both of his hands over the head of the Pipe keeper, the palms downward and fingers outstretched and close together. He does not touch the head of the Pipe keeper with his hands. In this position he bows his head and makes a silent prayer, of his own choice, in which Friday, who is standing on his left, joins. When "he who covers the Pipe" raises his head and lowers his hands the prayer is concluded and the Pipe keeper signs to him and the rest of his party to take seats along the south wall of the tent. All do so, taking the seats pointed out to them by the Pipe keeper. The women who carry the food bring it as far as the door of the tent, where it is then taken by Luke Smith, assistant keeper, and placed on the ground in the middle of the tent.[3]

Along the south wall of the tent, all facing north, are seated the following: In the southwest corner of the tent is seated Pete White Plume, alternate keeper; on his right is seated Robert Friday, chairman of the Arapaho tribal council; on his right is "he who covers the Pipe"; on his right is seated his wife, and on her right his daughter; on her right is Mrs. Elkin, and on her right is Mr. Elkin, and on his right is seated Vic Fontenelle, who is at the southeast corner of the tent, next to the door. In this line all, save Pete White Plume, belong to the party of "he who covers the Pipe." Seated along the north wall of the tent and facing south are the following: In the northwest corner of the tent is Carry Shot Gun, helper; on his left is George White Antelope, helper; on his left is seated Pete L. Brown, helper; on Brown's left is a Southern Arapaho visitor, whose name could not be ascertained; on the visitor's left is Esau Grasshopper, helper; and on his left, seated nearest to the door, is Yellow Calf, helper. There are, in all, five helpers and one Southern Arapaho visitor (Friday). The visitor came to Wind River with three bus loads of Southern Arapaho who made a 3 days' journey from Oklahoma to see the Northern Arapaho sun dance. He is greatly pleased to be present here and see the Flat Pipe, which he had never hoped to see, and he takes occasion at the proper time in the ceremony to express his appreciation and thanks to "he who covers the Pipe." Along the west wall of the tent, and facing east, are: Oscar White, keeper of the Flat Pipe, who is seated directly in front of the west tent pole and the Flat Pipe bundle; on his left is seated Luke Smith, assistant keeper, and his stepson; on his right is seated Lizzie White Plume, woman helper to the Pipe keeper (Friday). There are 17 persons present altogether. Shave Head states that he and his wife sometimes assist Oscar White in the Flat Pipe ceremonies, and that Mrs. Yellow Bear, Oscar White's niece, often assists as woman helper, and that Chester Yellow Bear [4] sometimes takes the place occupied in the present ceremony by Pete White Plume. Both Pete White Plume and Chester Yellow Bear, who is not present at this ceremony, may be helpers. Friday states

---

[3] At this point the Pipe keeper looks over the food offerings and decides whether to give the complete ceremony, entirely exposing the Flat Pipe, or to give the ceremony in abbreviated form, by opening the bundle wrappings and affording those assembled only a brief glimpse of the Pipe resting in the bundle wrappings. This decision is entirely within the discretion of the keeper, and he need communicate his intended course to no one. In the ceremony here described the Flat Pipe was completely exposed and the entire ritual was given. This according to Robert Friday.

[4] Chester Yellow Bear is now (1938) assistant to Luke Smith, the Pipe Keeper (Friday).

that Lizzie White Plume is not related to Oscar White, but was called in because of her knowledge and skill in conducting the part of the ceremonies assigned to her. The fact that the assistant keeper, Luke Smith, is related to Oscar White, and is to be his successor, supports the statement (Mooney, 1896, p. 959) that this Pipe is handed down and kept only in a certain family of the Northern Arapaho. A diagram showing the lay-out of the tent and the positions of the various persons present is here appended (fig. 8).

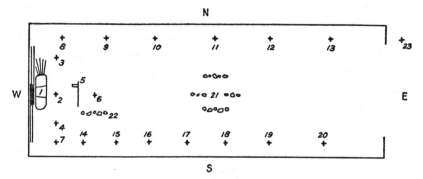

FIGURE 8.—Seating of persons in the tent where the ceremony took place.

1. Flat Pipe bundle slung on its stand. 2. Oscar White, keeper of Flat Pipe. 3. Luke Smith, assistant to keeper of Flat Pipe. 4. Lizzie White Plume, woman helper. 5. Pipe with catlinite bowl, brought in by "he who covers the Pipe." 6. Incense smudge. 7. Pete White Plume, alternate keeper and helper. 8. Carry Shotgun, helper. 9. George White Antelope, helper. 10. Pete L. Brown, helper. 11. A Southern Arapaho guest. 12. Esau Grasshopper, helper. 13. Yellow Calf, helper. 14. Robert Friday, instructor and interpreter to "he who covers the Pipe." 15. John G. Carter, "He who covers the Pipe." 16. C. C. Carter; 17. M. E. Carter; 18. Mrs. Elkin; 19. Mr. Elkin; 20. Mr. Fontenelle, of the party of "he who covers the Pipe." 21. Food brought in for the feast. 22. Food brought in for feast placed before woman helper to be blessed. 23. Woman on lookout before the door of the tent.

THE BLESSING BY THE TURTLE

When all are seated the keeper takes the pipe brought in to him by "he who covers the Pipe" from its place across his knees and puts it on the ground before him. It is laid pointing north and south, the bowl being to the north. The keeper then reaches into a bag at his right hand, which is made of buckskin and painted red, and takes out a turtle. The upper and lower shells of the turtle are painted red. The head of the turtle projects slightly from the shell, as do the paws. The head and the paws are of a hard, stony substance. The daughter of "he who covers the Pipe" observed that there seemed to be seeds inside the turtle shell, or else pebbles, as the turtle rattled when moved suddenly. The turtle appears to be an ordinary mud turtle. It is stated that this is the turtle who went down under the water to get the mud with which the earth was made in the beginning, according to the origin myth (Friday). The turtle was not taken from the Pipe bundle, as has been noted. The Pipe bundle is not opened until later in the ceremony.

The turtle is passed from hand to hand until it reaches Vic Fontenelle, who is seated at the southeast corner of the tent, near the door. Instructions are now given on how to handle the turtle, both by Oscar White, the keeper, and Luke Smith, his assistant. These instructions are interpreted by Robert Friday.

The turtle is first grasped with the left hand and is passed up the inner side of the right leg, from the ankle upward, and then up the body to the heart, and is pressed for a moment against the heart. Still grasped with the left hand, the turtle is then run up the right arm, from the wrist to the shoulder, and then across the body to a point over the heart, and is pressed for a moment against the heart a second time. It is then moved across the forehead with a semicircular motion and is transferred to the right hand. Some of the Arapaho made this semicircular motion over their heads, and by some this motion was gone through after the turtle had been transferred from the left hand, the motion being done with the right hand. The turtle when grasped in the right hand is then passed up the left arm, from wrist to shoulder, and across the body to a point over the heart, and is pressed for a third time against the heart for a moment. The turtle is then passed up the inner side of the left leg, from the ankle upward, and then up the body to the heart, where it is pressed for a moment for the fourth time. The turtle is then taken in both hands, the head is bowed, and the head of the turtle is held close to the lips, and four deep inhalations are made. Some of those present, including the keeper, held the turtle's head between their lips while making these four inhalations. When this has been concluded the turtle is passed with the right hand to the person directly on the left, who takes the turtle with his left hand, and in turn goes through the motions which have been described. The turtle thus travels clockwise around the tent, Vic Fontenelle, sitting south of the door and on the extreme east of the line along the south wall of the tent, receiving it first, and Yellow Calf, sitting north of the door, and on the extreme east of the line along the north wall of the tent, receiving it last. This ceremony is in the nature of a blessing (Friday). The purpose of the ceremony is probably to gain power and vital essence from this holy object.

PAINTING OF THE PARTY OF "HE WHO COVERS THE PIPE"

Luke Smith, assistant keeper, now rises from his place and leaves the tent, taking with him a paddle with which to carry live coals. He returns shortly with a live coal on the paddle and places the coal in front of Oscar White, the keeper. The coal is placed between the catlinite pipe that lies before the keeper and the door, but within easy reach of the keeper. Just before the coal is brought in "he who covers the Pipe" and all his party remove their shoes and stockings at the request of the keeper. They remain thus barefooted until almost the end of the ceremony.

Red paint, from a skin bag which is painted red, is now procured by Luke Smith and by Lizzie White Plume, the woman helper. They proceed to break off pieces of the red paint and mix it with tallow between the palms of their hands. The turtle is meanwhile restored to the keeper, who puts it back in its bag on his right. The keeper now takes up a smaller bag from which he takes a pinch of a reddish powder between the thumb, index, and middle finger of his right hand. The reddish powder is incense. The keeper makes five feints with the pinch of incense downward and over the catlinite pipe which lies before him. He then makes five feints with the pinch of incense over the live coal which lies just beyond the pipe. He deposits the incense upon the live coal. While doing this he recites a prayer in an undertone. It is to be noted that no prayer is said out loud throughout these ceremonies, and no songs are sung. Most prayers are uttered silently, or recited in an inaudible tone. The feints with the incense are said to be made to the four directions and to "above" (Friday). The incense is composed of cedar and castor among other ingredients, but all of the ingredients which go into the incense can only be learned by undergoing the 3-day fast and hearing the story of the Pipe and all that appertains to it from the keeper during the three nights of the fast (Friday).

As the smoke is arising from the incense Luke Smith, holding the paint which he has just mixed between the palms of his hands, and with the palms held close together, fingers extended and touching each other, extends his hands over the smoke of the incense. He first holds his hands with the back of the right hand down toward the smoke and then the back of the left hand to the smoke. Again he holds the back of his right hand to the smoke and again the back of his left hand. He then presents his hands to the smoke still held in their original position, but so that the sides with the little fingers are down toward the smoke. It will be observed that the usual four motions, and then a fifth, are gone through in passing the hands holding the newly mixed red paint through the incense. When Luke Smith has done this Lizzie White Plume does likewise with the red paint which she has just mixed. They are now ready to paint "he who covers the Pipe" and his party. Friday, "he who covers the Pipe," Elkin, and Vic Fontenelle are painted in turn by Luke Smith. The women of the party, consisting of the wife and daughter of "he who covers the Pipe" and Mrs. Elkin, are painted by Lizzie White Plume (fig. 9).

The person to be painted sits close to the person who is applying the paint, and with feet extended. The painting begins with the feet. Five dots of paint are applied to the feet with the ball of the thumb of the painter. The right foot is painted first and then the left foot. The first dot is applied to the instep, then near the arch, then the arch, then below the ankle, and finally the ankle. In the case of "he who covers the Pipe" a stripe was run up the outside of the leg on the trousers. The hands and wrists are painted next. The painter grasps both hands of the person to be painted with both of his hands and applies the spots of paint with the balls of his thumbs simultaneously. A spot of red paint is applied to the palms of the hands, then to the fatty part at the base of the thumbs, than at a point between thumb and index finger, then on the backs of the hands near the wrists, and finally on the wrists. In the case of "he who covers the Pipe" a

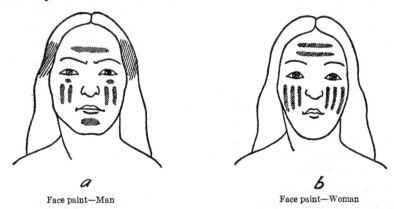

a   b
Face paint—Man   Face paint—Woman

FIGURE 9.—Painting of the party with "he who covers the Pipe." Body paint, men and women; on feet five spots made with ball of thumb by person applying paint. These spots begin on inner side of arch of foot, out over arch and up toward ankle. On the hands the paint consists of five red spots applied with ball of thumb of the painter, and start on palmar surface, near heel of hand, then over fatty portion at root of thumb, and up toward wrist from point between thumb and index finger. "He who covers the Pipe" had two stripes run up each pants leg and each sleeve, and two spots on the shirt, one above each nipple. The others reported that they did not get this extra attention. On men paint is also applied to hair on each side of head by painter pressing palms of his hands to both sides of the head of the man painted at the same time.

line of red paint was run up each forearm on the outer side and over the shirt and coat sleeves. Also a spot of paint was placed, in his case, above each breast upon the shirt. The face is painted next. With the men the chin is painted first; then two lines drawn vertically down each cheek from below the eyes; above these lines a dot is placed just below each eye; and finally a horizontal line is drawn across the forehead. The painter's hands are then placed on each side of the head, thus coloring the hair. The women receive three stripes horizontally across the forehead and three vertical stripes down each cheek, but no paint is applied to the chin. The feet and hands of the women are painted in the same manner as that of the men, as far as could be observed. The painting is accompanied by no audible prayer and the paint is laid on without any particular care or precision, but the job is done in a speedy and workmanlike manner.

The women, who are painted by Lizzie White Plume near the southwest corner of the tent, retire directly to their places after being painted. The men, who are painted by Luke Smith near the northwest corner of the tent, after receiving the paint retire to their places, and in doing so pass between the incense coal and the food which is placed in the center of the tent. Oscar White, keeper; Luke Smith, assistant keeper; Lizzie White Plume, helper; and Pete White Plume (Friday), alternate keeper, are not painted and do not paint themselves. The five helpers and the Southern Arapaho visitor, who sit in line along the north wall of the tent, paint themselves with red paint. No particular design was noted in their painting, but they did rub their chins with the paint, and their cheeks and hair. They do not paint their hands or feet. Those who have received the red paint from Luke Smith and Lizzie White Plume cannot partake of the feast, but are fed ceremonially in a manner later described. When "he who covers the Pipe" and his party have all been painted, and have returned to their places, Oscar White and Luke Smith, through Robert Friday as interpreter, warn those who have received the paint that they must not wash the paint off with water until the next day. Otherwise, they say, it will rain hard. Oscar White relates that once an Arapaho attended this ceremony and did not heed the warning given him, and washed the sacred paint from his face with water right after the ceremony. He was drowned in a cloudburst the next day. But, Oscar White added, it is proper to remove the paint, if desired, with vaseline or some similar substance, and if done in that manner no harmful results will follow.

The paint is applied as a blessing to "he who covers the Pipe" and his party and it resembles the first earth which was brought up from under the water by the turtle when the world was created (Friday). In the Northern Arapaho sun dance the Pipe keeper was observed applying the first touches of the body paint to some of the dancers, and he followed somewhat the same method of painting as observed in this ceremony (Kroeber, p. 294). Luke Smith and Lizzie White Plume were observed, in mixing the paint, spitting in the palms of their hands. Whether this act is ceremonial, as it is in the Rabbit tipi of the Southern Arapaho sun dance (Dorsey), or is simply to hasten the mixing of the paint, could not be ascertained.

SOCIABLE SMOKING

As before noted, in addition to the catlinite pipe brought in by "he who covers the Pipe" which lays before the keeper, Friday has brought with him a pipe with a black stone bowl and a supply of tobacco mixed with kinnikinnick in a bag. This pipe is used for sociable smoking, although certain ceremonial forms are followed in this smoking also.

The pipe is passed stem up, the bowl forward and away from the body, and is passed with one hand. Sometimes the pipe is passed with the bowl toward the body, but the stem is always upward, and at an angle. The pipe is filled and lighted by Friday, who passes it to the man on his left, who smokes, and the pipe is thus smoked down the line, following a clockwise direction, until it reaches Yellow Calf, who sits just north of the door. He smokes, and then the pipe is passed from hand to hand back to Friday, who fills and lights it again as often as is necessary. "He who covers the Pipe" and his party do not join in this smoke. Lizzie White Plume smokes the pipe in her turn. Friday says that this smoking will continue until the supply of tobacco he has brought is exhausted. He has gauged the time of the ceremony and his supply of tobacco well, as his tobacco gives out just before the end of the ceremony. The smoking of this pipe continues throughout the meal, which is eaten later. This is the only occasion among the Arapaho where it is considered proper to smoke a pipe during the course of a meal (Friday).

BLESSING OF THE FOOD

Luke Smith now brings forward a dish, receptacle, or pot containing some of each of the foods brought in for the feast, and places these before Lizzie White Plume, the helper. Lizzie White Plume obtains two can openers, which are taken from the bag which contains the turtle. With these the canned goods are opened and their contents poured into separate containers. There must be at least five varieties of food for this feast, and the greater additional varieties of foods provided the better the feast is considered for this ceremony, according to Arapaho standards. It is stated that the feast here provided measures up to the best Arapaho standards (Friday). Among other things which have been provided are bread, crackers, tea, coffee, boiled meat, gravy, tomatoes, vegetable soup, meat soup, canned peaches, canned pears, stewed apples, stewed berries, and a dish of boiled rice with raisins. A receptacle containing each of these dishes is now placed within arm's reach of Lizzie White Plume, who now takes from a bag some black powder. The ingredients of this powder are not known, and can only be learned by making the 3-day fast necessary to gain other information in regard to the Flat Pipe (Friday). The black powder is used in the blessing of the food. The procedure followed in blessing each receptacle of the food, including bread and crackers, tea, coffee, and soup, is the same. Lizzie White Plume takes a pinch of the black powder from the bag, which is small, made of buckskin, and painted red, and holding the powder between the tips of the thumb and the index and middle fingers of her right hand and praying silently, places a pinch of the powder in the food contained in one of the receptacles before her. The first pinch of the powder is put in the food in the east part of the receptacle. A pinch of the powder is then placed in the food in the south part of the receptacle, and then in the west, north, and middle of the receptacle. A prayer is said, silently, during the placing of each pinch of powder. This is done to the food in each of the containers which have been placed before Lizzie White Plume, and these containers have every variety of food which has been brought in for the feast. The other containers of food remain in the center of the tent as before. They hold only duplicates of the foods placed before Lizzie White Plume. These acts are intended as a blessing and consecration of the foods which have been brought in for the feast (Friday). While the food is being blessed Oscar White, the keeper, takes a horn spoon from the bag which holds the turtle and the can openers. The bag is at his right hand. The spoon appears to be very old. The keeper then takes some black paint, and using the index finger of his right hand as a paint brush, proceeds to decorate the spoon. Two lines are drawn from the lip of the bowl of the spoon, on each side of the bowl, the four lines extending down into the bowl, but not quite to its deepest point. In the center of the bowl, about equidistant from the ends of the four lines, is painted a black dot. The keeper hands this spoon to Lizzie White Plume as soon as she has finished her blessing of the food. During the blessing of the food the flaps of the tent are closed and they are not rolled back again until after "he who covers the Pipe" has offered the food to the four directions, the above, the earth, and Pipe bundle.

OFFERING OF THE FOOD BY "HE WHO COVERS THE PIPE"

Lizzie White Plume now takes the spoon and dips a very smal morsel of food from the east side of one of the receptacles before her This she transfers to her left hand. She then dips small morsels o food from the south, west, north, and center of this receptacle, and transfers these morsels to her left hand. Samples of food are taken from each receptacle before her in the same manner. Minute quantities of the bread and crackers are broken off and placed in the spoon, five morsels of each being taken, following the same procedure observed with the other foods. Minute quantities of the tea and coffee and other liquids are taken up in the same way, and moisten the mixture of foods held in her left hand. The mixture thus obtained is kneaded carefully with the left hand and is then placed on the tip of the horn spoon held in the right hand. The spoon with its contents is now carefully handed to "he who covers the Pipe" by Lizzie White Plume. "He who covers the Pipe" leaves his place and takes his stand directly in front of the Pipe keeper, between the catlinite pipe which lays before the keeper and the incense smudge. He stands with his back to the keeper, facing east. The incense smudge is in front of him and the catlinite pipe behind him. He holds the spoon in his right hand, at arm's length, the arm at an angle of about 45 degrees. Robert Friday stands on his right to aid and instruct him in what to do. The spoon, held upward at arm's length, is pointed first to the southeast corner of the tent and given four slight upward motions. It is then pointed south of east, and is again given four slight upward motions. The spoon is then pointed due east, and a single strong upward motion is given it. By this motion the food is offered to the sky, or above. The spoon is then pointed north of east, and four slight upward motions are made with it. The spoon is finally pointed to the northeast corner of the tent, and four slight upward motions made with it. The contents of the spoon are then carefully taken from it and placed on the ground at a point northeast of the smudge, and within about a foot of it, and the spoon is handed to Robert Friday. "He who covers the Pipe" now takes a morsel of the food which he has deposited on the ground, between the middle and ring finger of his right hand, and turns west, facing the Pipe bundle. He moves close to the bundle, taking his stand north of the keeper, and between the keeper and Luke Smith. With both hands, palms down and fingers extended, but held close together, he strokes the Pipe bundle four times. In doing this the hands are held parallel, the thumbs being about 6 inches apart. The strokes are given from right to left, and are made slowly, carefully, and with great deliberation. "He who covers the Pipe" then turns east again and deposits the morsel of food held between his fingers on the food which he just deposited northeast of the smudge. He then returns to his place. The consecrated food has now been offered by "he who covers the Pipe" to the four directions, to above, to the earth, and to the Pipe bundle. The flaps of the tent are now opened.

PARTY OF "HE WHO COVERS THE PIPE" FED CEREMONIALLY

Luke Smith now comes forward and removes all of the food which has been blessed from in front of Lizzie White Plume, with the exception of the pan filled with boiled rice and raisins. The food which has been blessed is placed with the other food in the center of the tent. Luke Smith then returns to his place. Robert Friday then goes forward and squats down in front of the pan containing the rice and raisins. Lizzie White Plume dips the horn spoon which she has received from the keeper into the rice and raisins at the east side of the dish, being careful to include one raisin with the portion of rice dipped up with the spoon. Holding the spoon in her right hand, she extends it to Friday across the pan and Friday, without touching the spoon with either hand, sucks the contents from the tip of the spoon. While doing this he reaches out his right hand and strokes the inner side of Lizzie White Plume's right forearm, from the crook of the elbow to the wrist, four times. A portion of rice and a raisin is now dipped from the south side of the pan with the spoon and Friday consumes it as he did the first spoonful, stroking Lizzie White Plume's right forearm four times while so doing. The third portion of this food is taken from the west side of the pan and is consumed in the same manner and following the same ritual as the other two portions. The fourth portion of one raisin and some rice is taken from the north side of the pan and is likewise consumed by Friday while stroking Lizzie White Plume's forearm four times. The fifth and last portion is taken from the center of the pan and is consumed with the same ritual as the other portions. Each mouthful must be sucked in from the spoon in such a manner that the spoon is cleaned of its contents. "He who covers the Pipe" now takes his place before the pan and is fed in the same manner and goes through the same ritual as Friday, and the rest of his party follow him in turn. This is the only food eaten during this ceremony by those who have received the paint. The feeding with the rice and raisins of the party of "he who covers the Pipe" is "all the same as communion," and the stroking of the arm of Lizzie White Plume is to draw strength (Friday). The keeper appears to enjoy the efforts of "he who covers the Pipe" and some of his party when attempting to eat from the horn spoon. None were very expert at it except Robert Friday.

THE FEAST

Lizzie White Plume now takes dishes and cups from a place behind her on her left and passes them down the line to all those persons present who are entitled to eat the feast. These include all in the tent except Friday and "he who covers the Pipe" and his party, who have received the paint. The food is then distributed, all taking whatever they wish, and using their pocket knives as eating utensils. The tea and coffee are served in the cups; the soups and gravy are not touched. The fruits are partly consumed. During the meal there is no conversation, and the pipe with the black stone bowl which Friday brought in is passed and smoked. As previously noted, this is the only occasion where it is considered proper among the Arapaho to smoke a pipe during the course of a meal (Friday). Friday and "he who covers the Pipe" and his party look on during the meal and smoke.

At the conclusion of the meal the keeper, his assistants, the helpers, and the Southern Arapaho visitor take what food they have left and tie it up in handkerchiefs to take home to their families. They do this, not on account of the food itself, but because the food has been blessed and offered to the four directions, the above, the earth, and the Pipe, and is therefore holy. Whoever eats this food is blessed, and receives health, long life, and good luck (Friday).

DISTRIBUTION OF FOOD

A discussion now follows, led by the Pipe keeper, in which some of the assistants and helpers join, as to who should receive the balance of the food. The five helpers and the Southern Arapaho guest take this occasion to thank "he who covers the Pipe" for the opportunity he has afforded them of attending this feast and ceremony. The Southern Arapaho guest is particularly sincere in his thanks, as he says he had never expected to look upon the Flat Pipe; that few Arapaho had ever seen it; that fewer still had given the ceremony and the feast; that he had just arrived after a 3-days journey by bus from Oklahoma, where the Southern Arapaho lived; and that now he could, when he returned to his people, tell them that he had looked upon the Flat Pipe.

It is finally decided to give the remaining food to four families, and their names are called out, summoning them to the tent. The women of these families come in and select such food as they wish and take it away with them. There is still some food remaining, which Luke Smith distributes, taking it to the door of the tent and handing it to certain women who come up to receive it. While the food is being distributed Lizzie White Plume takes the dish of rice and raisins before her, and the horn spoon, and after offering a portion of the dish, by placing a morsel upon the ground, proceeds to eat. When she has taken what she wishes, she passes the dish and spoon to the keeper on her left. He likewise offers a morsel on the tip of the spoon by placing it upon the ground in front of him, and then partakes of the dish. The dish then travels up the line to the left, the assistant, helpers, and the Southern Arapaho visitor eating from it as it comes to them. There is no other formality in the eating from this dish than the preliminary offering of a morsel by placing it on the ground, which has been noted. The dish is finally emptied by Yellow Calf, who sits on the north side of the tent, nearest the door. He passes the empty pan outside the door of the tent and the horn spoon is handed back down the line to Lizzie White Plume, who cleans it and hands it to the keeper. The keeper puts it back in its bag. All dishes, cups, and food containers are now passed outside the tent.

THE OPENING OF THE FLAT PIPE BUNDLE

Luke Smith leaves the tent and procures a live coal, which he brings in on an incense paddle and puts at the place of the smudge. Oscar White takes from the small leather bag a pinch of the incense, composed of cedar and castor. He holds it in his right hand, between the tips of his thumb, index, and middle fingers. He makes five feints with it over the catlinite pipe which lays before him, and then five feints over the live coal, meanwhile muttering a prayer. He places the incense on the live coal.

The Pipe bundle is hung from the four poles attached to the west tent pole in what appears to be an old saddlebag. The saddlebag has a fringe of red and white beads around its edge. The bag is enclosed around the bundle, and is secured by a leather strap with a buckle. An iron ring at one end of the strap serves to attach the strap to a leather thong. The other end of the thong is tied to the point of intersection of the four poles. The bundle is thus slung from the poles. The bundle is over 2 feet long and about a foot thick. From the north end of the bundle, as it hangs, five sticks protrude from under its outer wrapping of blue felt cloth. Eagle feathers are attached to the ends of these sticks. These feathers attached to their sticks are called the headdress of the turtle. The mouthpiece of the Pipe is called the head of the turtle (Friday). As the bundle hangs the mouthpiece of the Pipe, or head, points north, and is located under the headdress of the turtle. The bowl of the Pipe points south.

Rising from his place at the keeper's left, Luke Smith unties the thong which secures the bundle to the intersection of the four poles and takes the bundle down. He removes the saddlebag which acts as a cradle in which the bundle is slung, and places the bundle directly in front of the Pipe keeper. The bundle lies between the keeper and the catlinite pipe. The saddlebag is placed near the west wall of the tent, to the left of the keeper. All present are now very silent and attentive. Luke Smith removes the five sticks to the ends of which the eagle feathers are attached and which form the headdress of the turtle, and places them behind him, near the west wall of the tent. These sticks were drawn from between the outer wrapping of the bundle and the next wrapping. The outer wrapping of the bundle is secured by five rawhide thongs. These thongs are now untied by Oscar White and Luke Smith, and when removed are placed to one side. The outer wrapping is allowed to fall open and is not removed from under the bundle. The same holds true of all the other wrappings of the bundle, which are opened but not removed. A second wrapping is exposed by the opening of the first wrapping. It is of blue felt cloth like the first, and is tied in place by a long hair rope. The rope ends in a noose, which is secured around the bundle at its south end, or over the bowl of the Pipe. The rest of the rope is wound tightly around the bundle in five or six turns. Luke Smith unties the rope, unwinds it from around the bundle, and places it to one side. The second covering is thus allowed to fall open, and is not removed from under the bundle. By this time Luke Smith is perspiring considerably. The opening of the second wrapping discloses a third wrapping of red felt. This is tied in place by an ordinary piece of rope, which ends in a noose. The noose is around the south end of the bundle, over the bowl of the Pipe, and is then wound tightly around the bundle in five turns. This rope is removed from the bundle by Luke Smith and is placed to one side. The red felt cloth is opened but is not removed from under the bundle. A wrapping of yellow felt cloth is now disclosed, which is not secured in place by any binding. This is simply spread aside, disclosing the next wrapping, which appears to be composed of two wolf or coyote skins. These skins seem to be very old, the inner sides of the skins being deeply grooved or cracked, the hair being of a yellow tinge but in a good state of preservation. Information about the animals that furnished these skins, the history of the skins and of the other wrappings of the bundle, can only be told at night to a person making the proper 3-day fast when acquiring the story of the Pipe and other information relating to it (Friday). All matters pertaining to the history of the Pipe, its ritual, and the objects connected with the Pipe, can be spoken of only at night, and never in the daytime. In the old days, when the Pipe was smoked, it could be smoked only at night (Friday).

When the skins are unfolded Lizzie White Plume and several of the helpers bow their heads. The Southern Arapaho visitor and other helpers and "he who covers the Pipe" and his party are watching the proceedings with close attention. All those in the tent are very serious. The keeper now wipes his eyes, as though wiping away tears. The opening of the two skins discloses a wrapping of black silk. This in turn is spread apart, disclosing another wrapping of flowered silk. When this wrapping is spread apart, another wrapping of yellow silk is disclosed. This wrapping is carefully spread apart, disclosing the Flat Pipe, which is now resting on all of its wrappings.

As it lies in the bundle the bowl of the Flat Pipe points south, and its head, or mouthpiece, points north.

DESCRIPTION OF THE FLAT PIPE

The Flat Pipe is all of one piece. It is not divided into sections or parts. It appears to be made of stone, which resembles in color a yellowish sandstone, with a tinge of red.[5] It looks narrower and smaller when laid in its wrappings than it does when removed from the bundle. Viewed as it lies in its wrappings, it looks very flat. The Arapaho say the Flat Pipe is of stone (Shave Head; Friday; also Mooney, 1898, pt. 1, p. 242). Dr. Tyler, who was permitted to lift the Flat Pipe, says it is made of wood (Fontenelle). A close scrutiny of the Pipe shows no wood grain, and on being touched with the sole of the foot later in the ceremony it did not feel like wood. Fontenelle, who also saw the Pipe and touched it with his foot, believes that the Pipe is not made of wood. The color of the Flat Pipe is its natural color. It has not been painted (Friday).

---

[5] It appeared to be reddish yellow in color to two observers present at the ceremony. To the author it appeared a light mahogany in color. Robert Friday says the Flat Pipe is slate colored, but he examined the drawing of the Flat Pipe submitted with this paper, and appeared satisfied with it insofar as it showed the shape of the Flat Pipe.

When the Flat Pipe is removed from its bundle its appearance at first glance is one of great weight and crudeness in execution. It looks clumsy and awkward. The bowl seems of great size and weight in comparison with the stem. The Pipe looks thick and heavy. But a closer examination reveals that the carving of the Pipe is excellent and its lines are graceful. The head, near the mouthpiece, which is the head of the turtle, is well executed, as are the eyes in the head. The curve in the body, which is the stem of the Pipe, is well modeled and graceful. There is an overhanging lip around the outer rim of the bowl of the Pipe, and the bowl when looked at from above is square.

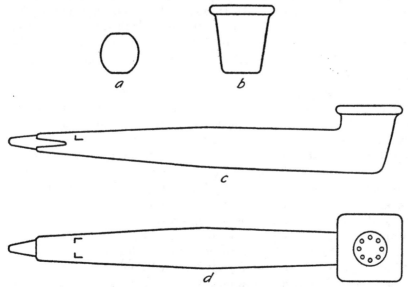

FIGURE 10.—Flat Pipe, Northern Arapaho. *a*, Section through stem. *b*, Front view of bowl. *c*, Side view of pipe. *d*, View of pipe from above. Description: Pipe is in one solid piece. Gives appearance of great crudeness, weight, and bulk, but is handled by its keeper as if very light. Color is light yellow. Dr. Tyler, missionary, who lifted it, says it is made of wood. Indians say it is stone. It looks like stone. Shows no grain. Might be tufa or pumice, or some like materia   Friday says it is sealed with tallow. There are small brass-headed tacks around edge of sealing substance near lip of bowl.

The opening in the bowl is sealed with a substance which is of the same color as the rest of the Pipe, and around the outer edge of this seal the heads of a number of brass tacks are embedded. These heads are very small. The Pipe is about 15 inches in length, by estimate. It is said by some to be about a foot long (Shave Head; Friday; Fontenelle). The keeper, who is an old man, and seems not very strong, lifts the Pipe as though it were very light.

The head, or mouthpiece, of the Pipe looks more like the head of a duck than the head of a turtle. But it is insisted that it is the head of a turtle (Friday). An Arapaho named Adopted has stated that the head of the Flat Pipe resembled the head of a duck (Dorsey and Kroeber, IV). A drawing of the Flat Pipe, made from memory on the day of the ceremony, is attached to this account (fig. 10).

INCENSING OF THE FLAT PIPE

Now the keeper lifts the Flat Pipe from its bundle, holding it carefully and reverently with both hands. His right hand is extended forward, under the Pipe near its bowl, and his left hand is holding the Pipe under its stem, near the head of the turtle. In lifting the Pipe from the bundle it is observed that neither the head of the turtle nor the bowl of the Pipe is either elevated or depressed, but the Pipe is held parallel to the ground. The Pipe is now held with the bowl forward, and away from the body of the keeper, the mouthpiece being next to the keeper's body. The bowl is held in the smoke that is rising from the incense smudge. It is moved through the smoke five times. This is done with great deliberation and care, so there is ample opportunity to obtain a good view of the whole Pipe. Lizzie White Plume, Luke Smith, and some of the helpers are now sitting with heads bowed. The others are gazing intently at the Pipe. No prayer is uttered audibly by the keeper.

Although the tent flaps are open there are no curious spectators around the door. This has been true thoughout the entire ceremony. Only those come to the tent who are summoned there. Others stay away from the tent. A couple of boys who chanced to pass close to the entrance earlier in the ceremony and looked in over their shoulders as they passed were ordered away by Yellow Calf, and left immediately. One, and sometimes two, women have been sitting near the door, outside the tent near its northeast corner, throughout the ceremony, and appear to be keeping a lookout. But none of the Indians have come near the tent except those who are called for.

After the bowl of the Flat Pipe is incensed the keeper lays it back on the bundle. But now it is laid with the bowl to the north, and the mouthpiece, or head of the turtle, to the south. In this position it lies parallel and bowl-to-bowl to the catlinite pipe which is between the Flat Pipe and the smudge. It is not observed when the Pipe was turned to its new position whether it was swung around clockwise or not. It was observed, however, that the bowl of the Flat Pipe was always held away from the keeper's body, while the mouthpiece of the Pipe was always held next to the keeper's body.

TOUCHING THE FLAT PIPE

The Pipe keeper now beckons to Robert Friday to come forward. Friday is barefooted, as are the rest of the party of "he who covers the Pipe." Friday leaves his place and steps up on that part of the Pipe bundle which lies between the Flat Pipe and Oscar White, the keeper. He faces north. He steadies himself by grasping two of the poles that are used as a stand for the pipe with his left hand. These poles are lashed to the west tent pole, slanting south at an angle from the tent pole, and lie flat against the west wall of the

CARTER] THE NORTHERN ARAPAHO FLAT PIPE   97

tent. Friday now places the sole of his bare right foot on the Flat
Pipe, down near the mouthpiece or head of the turtle. He lifts his
foot and then places it down on the Flat Pipe on the stem near the
head of the turtle. He lifts his foot and then places it on the stem of
the Pipe near its bowl. He then places his foot on the bowl of the
Flat Pipe. In each instance the foot is placed down flat and squarely
on the Flat Pipe. The right foot is then placed on the Pipe bundle
just west of the Pipe bowl, and Friday then releases the grip of his
left hand on the two poles with which he has steadied himself and
brings his left foot up beside his right foot. To do this involves
almost stepping over the lap of the keeper. Friday then turns to his
right, around the head of the Pipe, and turning a second time, faces
south. He then returns to his seat, keeping the incense smudge on
his right and between himself and the keeper when so doing. "He
who covers the Pipe" now steps forward and follows the same procedure in placing his right foot on the Flat Pipe as did Friday. He is
followed in turn by the rest of his party, men and women, in the
order that they are seated along the south wall of the tent. Friday,
"he who covers the Pipe" and his party now put on their stockings
and shoes once more. The five helpers and the Southern Arapaho
visitor, who sit along the north wall of the tent, now remove their
footwear. They come forward each in turn, crossing to the south of
the tent, and keeping the incense smudge on their right, between
them and the keeper. They then turn north, step up to the Pipe
bundle, touch the Pipe four times with the sole of the right foot,
following the same procedure just described, and return to their places.
Oscar White, the keeper, Luke Smith, his assistant, and Lizzie and
Pete White Plume do not go through this ceremony, but remain in
their places. While the Pipe is being touched Lizzie White Plume
sits with her head bowed toward the Pipe.

Luke Smith now goes to the door of the tent and announces that all
who wish to may come in and see and touch the Pipe. Within a very
short time a large number of men, women, and children appear at the
door of the tent. All are barefooted. They cross the tent in single
file, crossing the tent along its south wall, in front of the party of
"he who covers the Pipe." They then turn north, step on the Pipe
bundle, touch the Pipe four times with their right foot as the others
have done, and then turn to the right and leave the tent. It will be
observed that they thus pass around the tent clockwise. There is
no loitering around the door of the tent by anybody. The small
children, who are unable, or do not know how to touch the Pipe, are
lifted across the Pipe with the assistance of Luke Smith and of the
women who bring them in. As they are thus lifted across the right
foot of the child is pressed down on the Pipe four times, in the proper
places, either by Luke Smith or the woman who has brought the child.

The purpose of this ceremony is to derive strength from contact with the Flat Pipe. Those who touch the Pipe four times with their right foot draw from the Pipe great strength, health, and long life (Friday).

The ear of corn, which is in the bundle, just below the Flat Pipe, is not taken out for this ceremony. Nor is "he who covers the Pipe" permitted to lift the Flat Pipe, or touch it in any other way than in the manner described. If the five sun shells had been presented to the Pipe keeper it would have been possible for "he who covers the Pipe" to actually lift the Flat Pipe (Friday).

WRAPPING OF THE FLAT PIPE BUNDLE

When all have touched the Pipe who wish to do so, Oscar White ifts the Flat Pipe carefully from the bundle, holding it as he did before, the right hand under the Pipe near the bowl and the left hand under the Pipe near the mouthpiece. He runs the bowl of the Pipe slowly and carefully through the smoke of the smudge five times. He then lays the Pipe back on its bundle in its original position; that is, with the bowl pointing south, and the mouthpiece, or head of the turtle, pointing north.

Each of the silk wrappings of the Flat Pipe are now carefully folded back over the Pipe and rewrapped in their turn by Oscar White. When he comes to the two skin wrappings it is again noticed that he wipes his eyes, as though brushing away tears. All are watching intently. The gesture of the keeper in wiping his eyes when unwrapping and wrapping the skins is believed to be no accidental gesture. He only wiped his eyes twice during the entire ceremony, and each time he did so was when touching these skins. The felt cloth wrappings are now each folded around the bundle in their turn, and their proper ropes and bindings brought out and each is secured around its proper wrapping. The same order is followed as when untying the bundle. Luke Smith ties the ropes, and is careful to secure them in place just as they were when the bundle was unwrapped, and to pull the ropes very tight. When the outermost cover is folded in place both Oscar White and Luke Smith join in tying the five leather thongs around it. After securing the outer wrapping Luke Smith takes up the five sticks which have the eagle feathers attached to their ends, the headdress of the turtle, and runs them carefully and one at a time in between the outer wrapping and the next wrapping of the bundle. The sticks are run in at the north end of the bundle and are put in far enough to leave some of the stick protruding beyond the end of the bundle, so that the eagle feathers hang free. The saddle-bag, which is used as a cradle with which to hang the bundle, is adjusted next. There is some difficulty about this. The cradle is adjusted three or four times by Luke Smith before Oscar White is satis-

fied that the bundle balances correctly in the cradle. At this point
Luke Smith is doing the work and Oscar White is doing the directing.

By now the tobacco and kinnikinnick mixture which Robert
Friday has brought with him to be smoked in his black stone pipe
has run out and the sociable smoking comes to an end. Luke Smith
picks up the Flat Pipe bundle by the ring attached to the strap and
ties it by a thong to the point of intersection of the four poles secured
against the west pole of the tent.

COVERING OF THE FLAT PIPE BUNDLE

Oscar White now picks up the catlinite pipe brought in by "he who
covers the Pipe." He takes it from the place where it has laid before
him throughout the ceremony and hands it to "he who covers the Pipe."
He holds the pipe in his right hand, bowl downward, and the stem
slanted at an angle of about 45 degrees. The stem is slanted toward
the keeper. "He who covers the Pipe" receives the pipe with his
right hand and rests the projecting end of the bowl on the ground.
The stem slants toward him, so that the mouthpiece is only a short
distance from his lips. He holds the pipe with his right hand. Friday
hands him a box of matches and "he who covers the Pipe" lights the
catlinite pipe and draws on it to get it well lighted. Keeping the pipe
lighted, he walks over to the keeper and sits on his heels before him.
The keeper takes the lighted pipe and wraps around it the blue felt
cloth offering which "he who covers the Pipe" brought in with him at
the start of the ceremony. The offering is folded around the stem of
the pipe. The pipe is now placed with the projecting end of its bowl
touching the ground and its stem slanted toward Oscar White, the
keeper. "He who covers the Pipe" grasps the pipe with his left hand
down near the bowl, and outside the cloth offering, to hold the offering
in place. The keeper grasps the pipe with his right hand, up near the
mouthpiece, the hand being outside the cloth offering to hold it in place
at that end of the pipe. The position of "he who covers the Pipe" is
southeast of the keeper, he and the keeper facing each other. The
keeper now takes four draws from the pipe, and at each draw "he who
covers the Pipe" strokes with his right hand the inner side of the right
forearm of the keeper, from the crook of the elbow down to the wrist.
"He who covers the Pipe" now removes the felt cloth wrapping from
around the pipe, being careful to do so in such a manner that it will
not disturb the position of the pipe or the grip of the keeper on the
stem of the pipe. "He who covers the Pipe" then unfolds the cloth
wrapping, with its present attached, the bill pinned to the cloth being
toward the Flat Pipe bundle. He then steps to the north of the keeper,
and in between him and Luke Smith, who sits at the keeper's left, and
stands close to the Flat Pipe bundle. Robert Friday stands on his
left. He now carefully spreads the blue felt cloth, the bill pinned

inside so as to be next to the bundle, and lays it over the bundle and smooths it out. Thus he covers the pipe. "He who covers the Pipe" now lays both hands upon the pipe bundle, palms down, fingers extended and touching, and thumbs about 6 inches apart. He then bows his head and utters a silent prayer, of his own choice, for a few moments. Friday, standing on his left, also utters a prayer. "He who covers the Pipe" and Friday then return to their seats.

The keeper smokes the catlinite pipe and passes it to Luke Smith on his left. The pipe is smoked, passing it to the left, until it reaches Yellow Calf, who sits north of the door of the tent on the extreme left. When Yellow Calf has smoked the pipe is passed from hand to hand until it again reaches Friday. Friday smokes, and passes the pipe to his left, and it is smoked down the line to the left a second time until it reaches Yellow Calf, who finishes the pipe. The empty pipe is then handed along the line until it is taken by Oscar White. At this time several talks are made by Yellow Calf and others. At the suggestion of Friday, "he who covers the Pipe" makes a short address. All of the talks are made seated.

CONCLUDING CEREMONY

While the talks are being made Oscar White proceeds to clean the bowl of the catlinite pipe. He first places the pipe before him, the projecting end of the bowl on the ground, and the stem upright, but slanting toward him. Holding the stem with his right hand, he mutters a prayer, and rubs earth from the ground before him with the fingers of his left hand, and he strokes the pipe up and down the left side with the fingers of his left hand. This is done twice. He then holds the pipe with his left hand, and still praying, rubs the ground with the fingers of his right hand, and strokes the right side of the pipe up and down with the fingers of his right hand. This is done twice. The keeper then holds the pipe to his right and cleans the ashes carefully from the bowl and deposits them on the ground. The ashes are shaken from the bowl a little at a time. After shaking the bowl four times it is empty. The last ashes are removed on the fourth shaking. When the pipe is empty the prayer ceases.

A fresh coal is brought in by Luke Smith and placed on the smudge before the keeper. The keeper takes the incense, made of cedar and castor, and holding a pinch between the thumb, index, and middle fingers of his right hand makes five feints with it over the coal. He then deposits the incense on the coal. He now hands the empty catlinite pipe to "he who covers the Pipe." In handing it he holds it with his right hand, bowl downward and forward, and the stem slanted upward at an angle of about 50 degrees. The stem slants toward the keeper. "He who covers the Pipe" takes the pipe with his right hand and rises. He then holds the empty pipe with his right hand forward under the bowl and his left hand under the stem near the mouthpiece. The bowl of the pipe is about level with the pit of the stomach. The stem slants to the left of the body and the pipe is held close to the body, the bowl slanted slightly downward. He now steps north, crosses over the incense smudge, then turns east and leaves the tent. Friday and the rest of his party follow him in order, each stepping over the incense smudge in front of the Pipe keeper. On leaving the tent the party turns south and breaks up just south of the tent.

The keeper, assistants, and helpers now leave the tent, with the exception of Luke Smith. Luke Smith takes down the Flat Pipe bundle from its place and unties the four poles from which the bundle is hung. He places these under his arm with the bundle and returns with them to the dwelling place of Oscar White.

This concludes the ceremony, which began at 11 o'clock in the morning and ended at 3 o'clock in the afternoon, consuming 4 hours.

REFERENCES CITED

CLARK, W. P.
    1885   The Indian sign language.   Philadelphia, 1885.
DORSEY, GEORGE A.
    1903   Arapaho Sun dance.   Publs. Field Columb. Mus., Anthr. Ser., vol.
           IV, Chicago, 1903.
DORSEY, GEORGE A., and KROEBER, A. L.
    1903   Traditions of the Arapaho.   Publs. Field Columb. Mus., Anthr. Ser.,
           vol. V, Chicago, 1903.
KROEBER, A. L.
    1902   The Arapaho.   Bull. Amer. Mus. Nat. Hist., vol. XVIII, New York,
           1902.
MOONEY, JAMES.
    1896   The Ghost-dance religion and the Sioux outbreak of 1890.   Four-
           teenth Ann. Rept. Bur. Amer. Ethn., pt. 2, Washington, 1896.
    1898   Calendar history of the Kiowa Indians.   Seventeenth Ann. Rept.
           Bur. Amer. Ethn., pt. 1, Washington, 1898.
    1907   [Article] Arapaho.   Bull. 30, Bur. Amer. Ethn., pt. 1, pp. 72–74,
           Washington, 1907.
STRONG, WM. DUNCAN.
    1935   Introduction to Nebraska archeology.   Smithsonian Misc. Colls., vol.
           93, no. 10, Washington, 1935.

INFORMANTS

Fontenelle, Victor.
Friday, Robert.
Friday, Mrs. Robert.
Roberts, Dr. John.

Shave Head.
Smith, Luke.
White, Oscar.

CPSIA information can be obtained
at www.ICGtesting.com
Printed in the USA
BVHW092152260421
605923BV00013B/382